The Wonders of the Environment

Clare Pillarkins

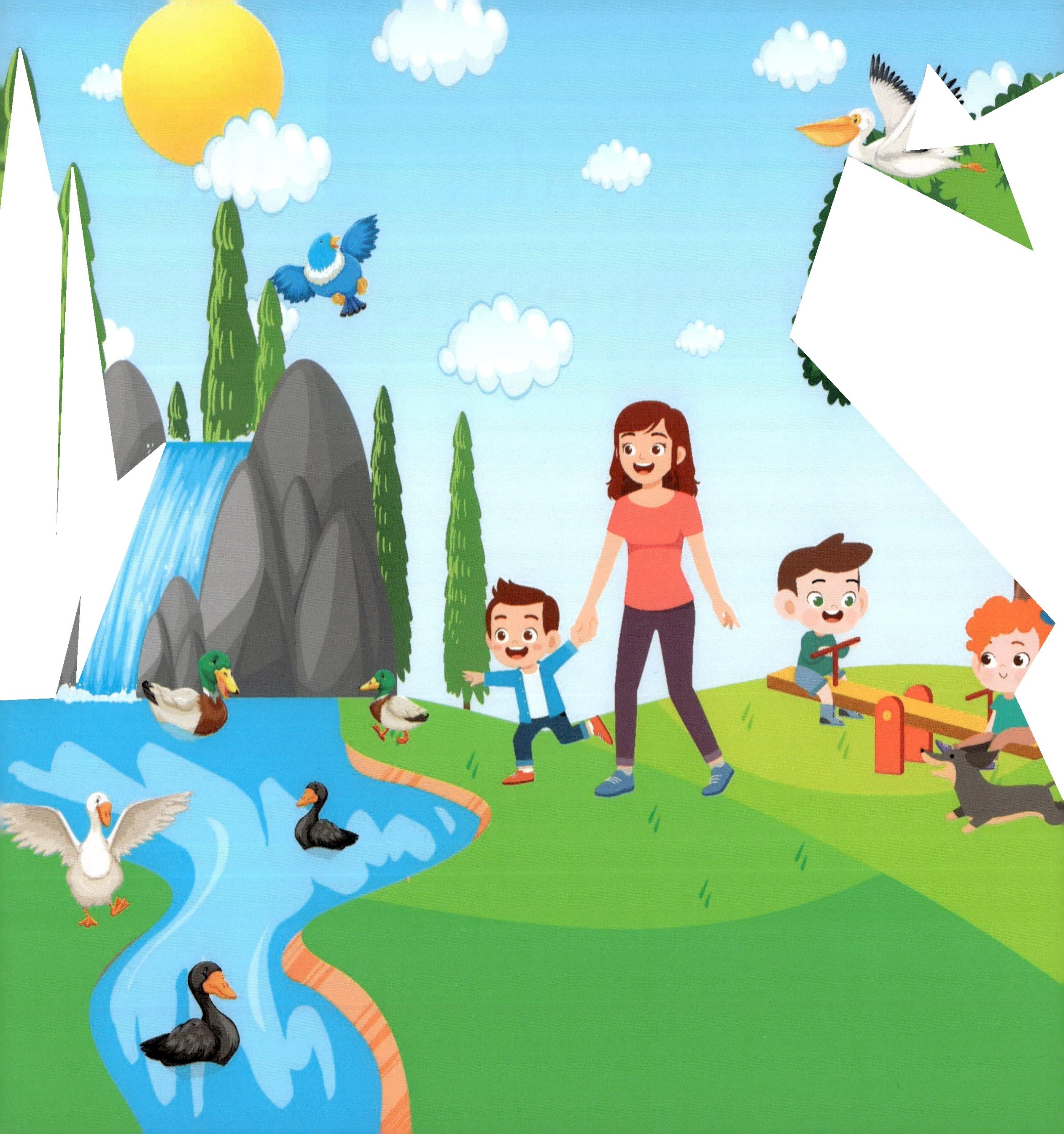

The environment is everything that surrounds us.

Living things like people, animals, and plants, are part of the environment.

Nonliving things like air, soil, water, stones, and the sun, are part of the environment.

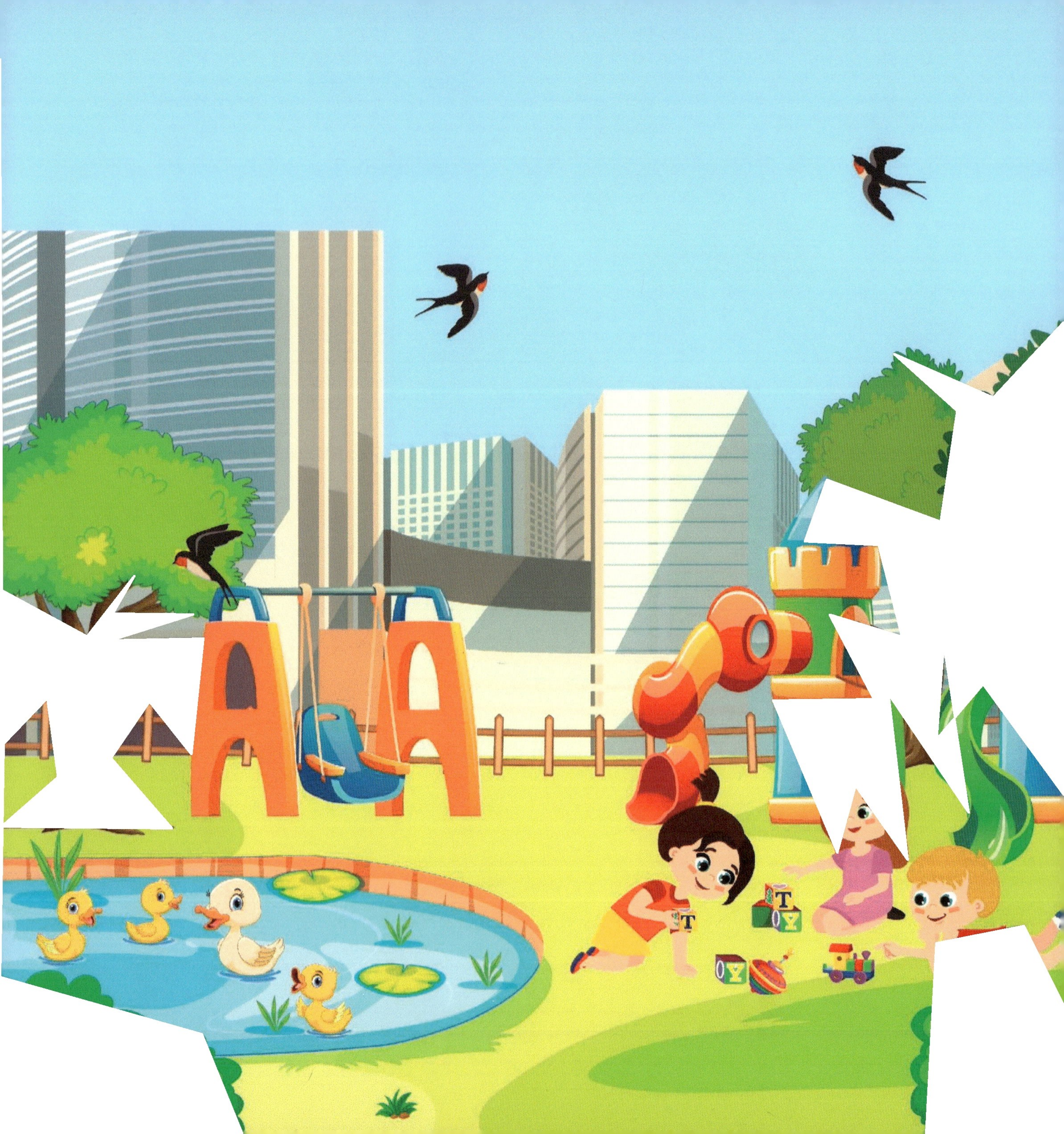

The environment gives us a lot of good things.

The environment gives us wonderful things.

Are you ready to see the wonders of the environment?

Wonder 1: The environment gives us air to breathe

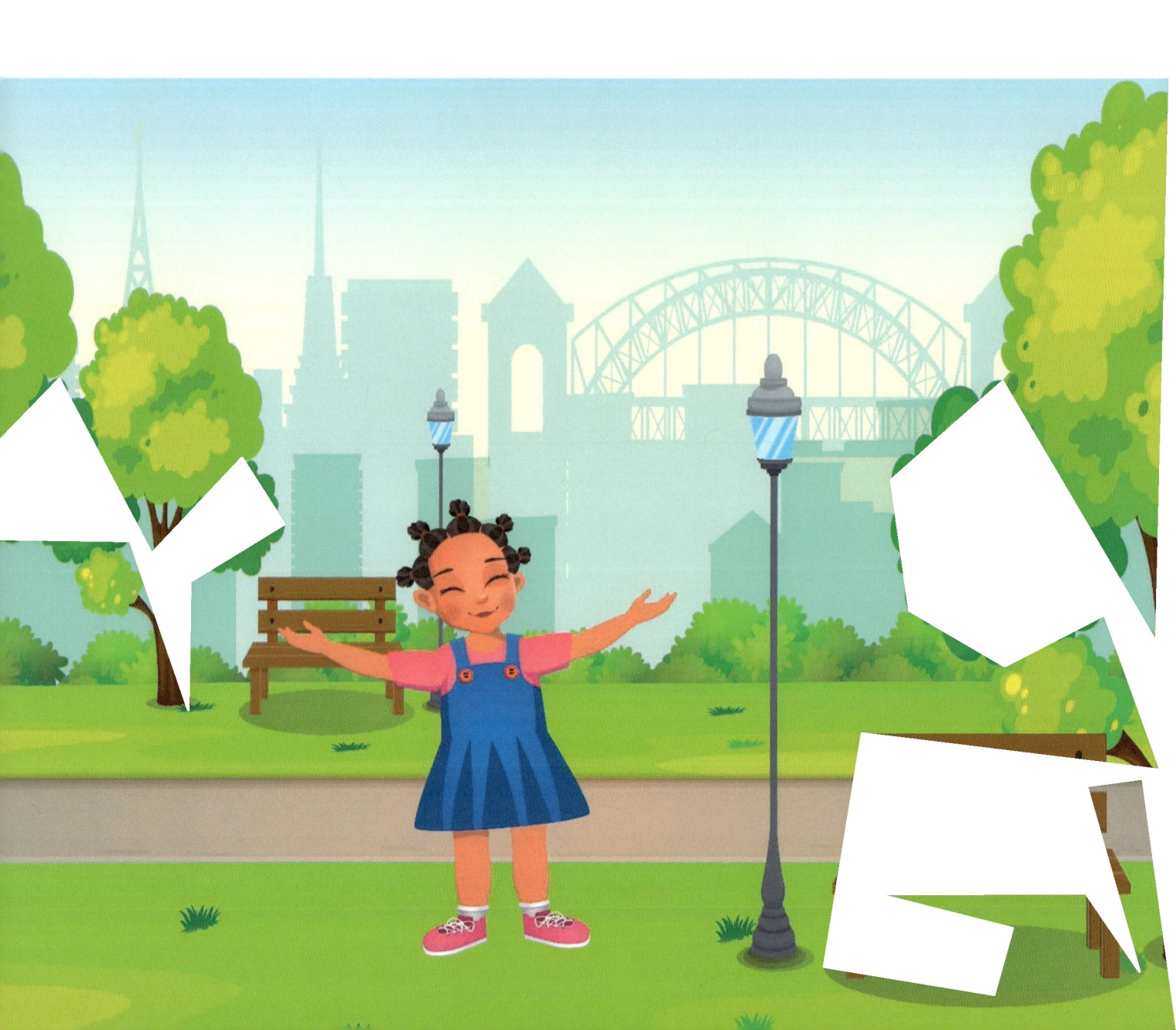

But if we do not take care of the environment, it might not be able to give us clean air anymore.

What should we do?

Trees give us air.
Let's plant a tree!

Wonder 2: The environment cleans the air we breathe

But if we do not take care of the environment, it might not be able to clean our air in future.

What should we do?

Trees clean the air.
Let's protect trees!

Wonder 3: The environment gives us water to drink

We need to take care of the environment so that we don't run out of water.

What should we do?

We will close the tap when brushing our teeth to save water!

Wonder 4: The environment gives us food to eat

We need to support the environment so that it can give us more food in future.

What should we do?

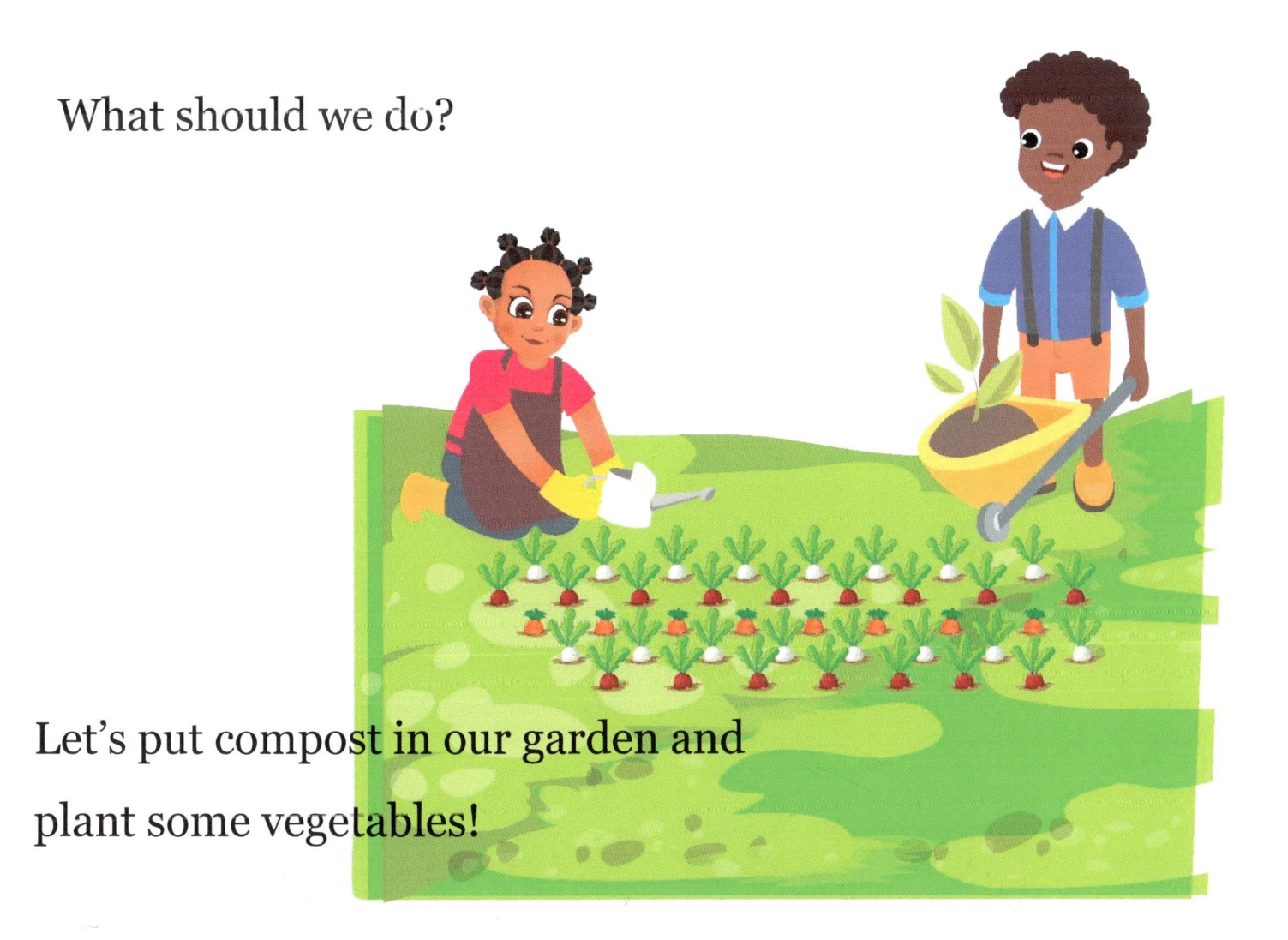

Let's put compost in our garden and plant some vegetables!

Wonder 5: The environment is our home

We need to keep our environment clean.

What should we do?

We will not litter!

Wonder 6: The environment gives us materials for items in our home

But if we don't take care, the environment can run out of these materials.

What should we do?

We will not ask for lots of new toys!

We will enjoy what we have because we are all different!

Wonder 7: The environment is home to wildlife

We need to protect the environment so that wildlife can have a home.

What should we do?

Let us save forests by practicing the **3Rs**!

Reduce waste! We will eat all the food on our plate.
Reuse waste! We will donate toys we don't use.
Recycle! We will set out bottles and cans so they can be turned into new products.

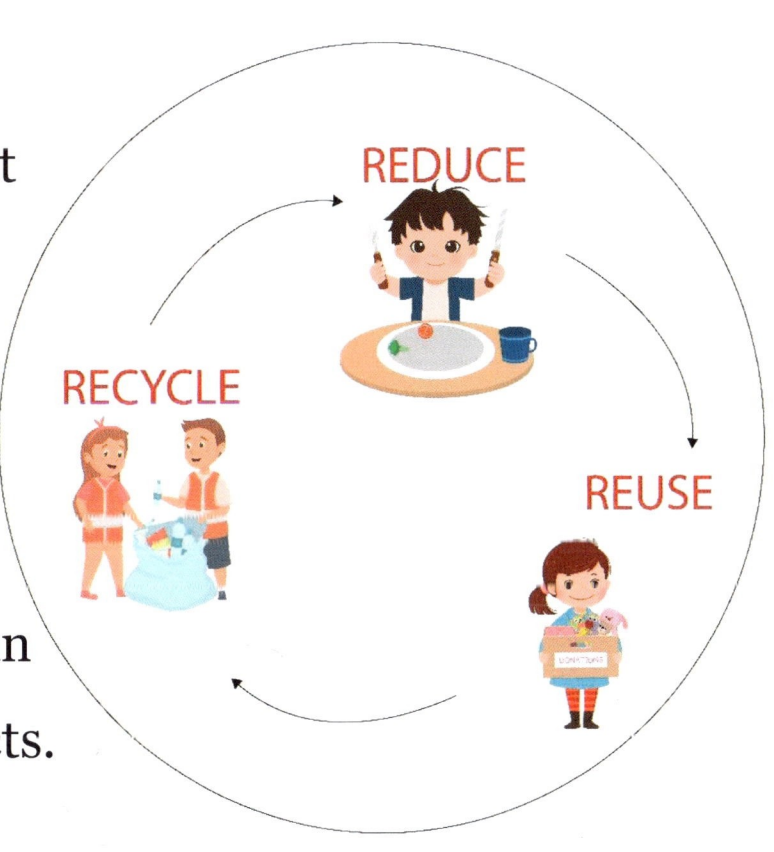

Wonder 8: The environment gives us energy for our homes

Let us make sure we don't run out of energy.

What should we do?

Our lights use up energy.

We will switch off the lights when leaving a room to save energy!

Wonder 9: The environment provides enjoyment to us

Let's enjoy the environment.

What should we do?

Let us play outdoors, it's so much fun!

Wow! There are so many wonders of the environment!

We love the environment!

We will protect the environment together!

Would you mind taking a minute to leave your feedback? Reviews from wonderful customers like you help other parents to feel confident about choosing this book as well.

Reviews also help me create better books and I will be very grateful.

Please, leave your review here:
http://www.amazon.com/review/create-review?&asin=B09B1XMMKF

Get "The Wonders of Rivers" Coloring Book for FREE!

Thank you for purchasing this Book! Did you already get your free coloring book? Get it here;

https://bit.ly/3cPQMCr

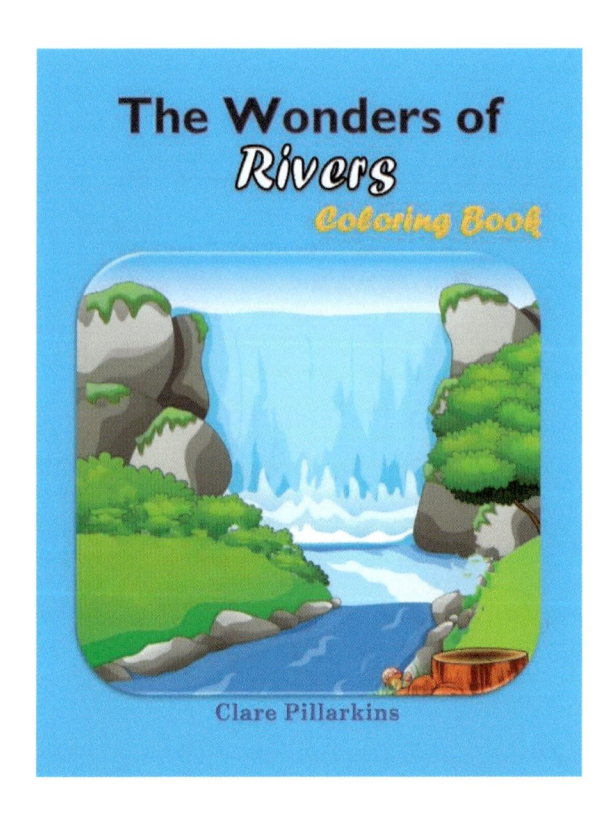

Other Books in this Series

The Wonders of Rivers
https://www.amazon.com/dp/B09MYTFXWK

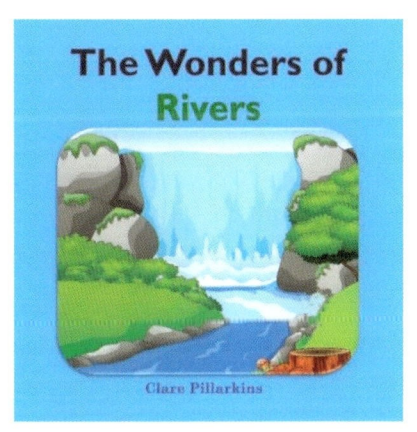

The Wonders of Lakes
https://www.amazon.com/dp/B09YDB58X5

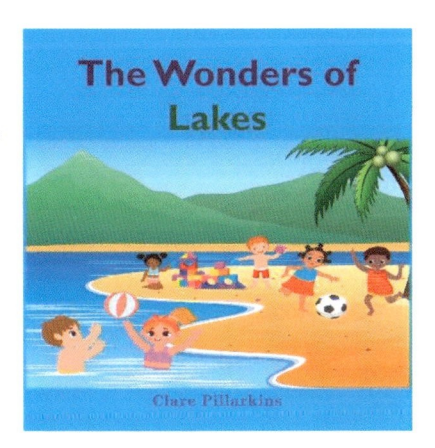

Printed in Great Britain
by Amazon

This book bclongs to:

Copyright © 2021 by Clare Pillarkins

All rights reserved. No part of this book may be reproduced in any form or by any electronic or mechanical means, including information storage and retrieval systems without written permission from the author, except in the case of a reviewer who may quote brief passages embodied in critical articles or in a review.